otherwise you well?

otherwise you well?

Richard Fox

ISBN 978-1-928476-40-5
ebook ISBN 978-1-928476-41-2

Published by Deep South
Makhanda, South Africa
contact@deepsouth.co.za
www.deepsouth.co.za

Distributed in South Africa by
Blue Weaver Marketing and Distribution
https://blueweaver.co.za

Distributed worldwide by
African Books Collective
PO Box 721, Oxford, OX1 9EN, UK
www.africanbookscollective.com/publishers/deep-south

Earlier versions of some of these poems
were published in *New Coin*

Cover painting: Quinten Edward Williams 'Crossing Over' (acrylic on canvas)
Cover design: Matt Reid and Robert Berold
Text design and layout: Liz Gowans

Contents

Global Village Idiot

Tech Tock
seems to me we're out of luck. Out of time. and Out of date.
Clearly, I heard calling from the rooftops. through the
satellite dishes, through the marshall amps,
unanimous calls for a reset. Back to the stone age. Back to
the copperwire age. Back to the telephonic ringtones
of the soul.

The best things in life are deepfried
gemstones. The ones in smart
gadgets. Life affirming affirmations. Not even facebook.
The next facebook. The facebook of robot lovers
and cartesian soldiers. The dynamite magnates,
the overlords, the geniuses behind the sellout.

I've been meaning to talk to you about this.
But I ran out of airtime.
It's a figure of speech in a new kind of language.
I got tickets to the sellout, I picked them up for a steal.
Everything you will ever want now has to be downloaded
from amazon rainforest. From the google jungle.
Using your genetic makeup applied without the help
of laboratory animals. Who are dead. As God is dead.
As democracy is dead. They all died
in the sellout.

It was a global redcarpet auction event attended not only
by the rich and the famous. But by every living being
with a coded stub, hooked into their heart at birth.
Planted there by extraterrestrial monkeys. Like in the movies.
I was there. I took pictures for the papers.
With a graphite pen stole your hearts, and
sold all the stubs for peanuts. What else could I do?
They are coming. And we are out of time.
Out of luck. And out of date.

I looked up on the internet. Saw all the stars had turned to dust
Around a giant masquerading wheel of flame. Every metal petal.
Every plastic vase in which our dreams were cast, are dashed.
Shattered into a handful of magnetic flares that lead the ever
hopeful on – global village idiots carving out their plans
in biomass. In scree. Along indecipherable journeys
between points that cannot join. You cannot join the sellout.
All the tickets are dead.

When last did I hear from you?

Animal mind is tripping blind across the bush elastic;
and the planetary sun, swept entirely upside down
lingers on the ripples of the tide.

When last did I hear from you? Last year's rains
are memory thin, tomorrow's mirror is a curved ruin

we build our bridges across rivers that no longer run.
Our endings and our beginnings
are no longer paired
we wander effortless through the seven dimensions.

Fields of wheat fields of mechanised precision;
the heartless rows of crows.
I've been burning both my footprints for hundreds of years
and still these roads do not close, still the borderguards.

Tethered fires
how many lengths of wood, how many
buckets of blood. How fast do we disappear
in dual rearview mirrors?

I've lost so much
more than I can understand. I refuse to accept
the child of your regret.
I leave it out with the morning papers
for the scavengers to collect. I detest

any real form of punishment
or neglect. I've grossed the tallies and set out the rallies
somewhere on the internet

Bullish Bearish. Amish
Lavish. The nuclear towers of Babel,
swing wide.

*

Frontal lobe, swift data carriers, the animal mind is tripping
glass bottle breakers, plastic chairs to the grand parade.

Rainbow chicken lottery tickets
with sharp, retractable claws.

Highlights will be shown at
midnight, Eastern Central Time.
I just got off the phone with Donald; I just got off
Melania, I just got off a plane from east
Texas, The robber barons and the bones, the endless
clatter of bones.

Stirling diamond glitterazzi, all the new paupers on display
fire and ice and graveyard dice, fast cars finish last.

*

Animal mind is tripping pure cerebral love;
The last bazaar in the everglades,
the oasis filters our dreams.

The borderguards are closed, borderpatrols have opened
on Nasdaq, everyone
is singing the song of the fear of their people

floating around on bubbles; coasting to a stop in the desert,
Turning the key, turning the screws,
waterboard championship riders of waves of future tech.

Animal mind is tripping great big breaker balls to the wall –
why are the waters rising on our planet;
why do we refuse to drink the medicine

I love you, phone charger, I love you
ice cream truck, I love you cold chain silicon implant,
I Love You, Miley Circus.

After the final broadcast from the bunkers of the leaders
of our enthusiasts, we chased dragons by their tails
we cornered the globetrotters
in their pens

and in the morning papers as the batteries held
the screens of the world
fired up one by one, like birdsong.

other people's music

this here's for the rest of us – the 7 & onehalf billion of us
rollingaround in slimcat alley, sucking the fatscum
off the ribbedconcrete sewergrates,
this here's my latest tune / my most important update
my one last swandance amongst the pigeons
with their tails up, and their pigeontoed whores?
looking on whitely, winely, brazenlyfuckdup
across the hemispheres rotund – you dig?
dig the master mashup? dig the cortex of
sound wound round your gooseneck throat?
dig the dogeared vandals of your fortyfoot float
listing away on the eldertides / carrying all your
jesuses out to sea; in swillage, in garbage,
in plastic fruitcakes and minceonion manacles,
and we leave those fuckers to drown hoho!
we leave them to sink to the bottom of the beaches,
where all the beaches were, where the whalessing
padre, where the whales sing for your harness
your safetycambelt fulllength feature down
the untoted roads of our collective upbringing –

just a light rinse of vomit through your gills
then ur into the clear, my son – my light –
my last vestige of cleangreendetergent
just one last fucking fling at the sun and then
you can take me home to sleep it off like a raven.

all our dressings are blessed
in blood
in cankers
in fools with their teethkicked
out; all our hopes are flooded
with wonder
with sails used to moor
the dead to their north
pointing poles,

and to wrap the living in
carhorn alarmbell eggshell
white white white white white ...

hanging along the margins of dawn
there are seventy ripped skeletons
with their muscles sinew stripped
by the hunched black crows,
hanging along the margins and the
crown; there are and there are
histories and theories and elegies
and clowns.

Not without this night I could pace across the desert
and eat the worms out of your ears my dears, not
without all your clinging forms and diseased boreholes
could I build castles out of bullshit – factories out of lies,
and without colliding stars I could leaven out your mind
heave your carcass across the line, dragging you
every inch of this way and guided blindly
by other peoples music

It doesn't mean anything / anyway

It doesn't mean anything – it's all
coming to an end. Temporarily
at least. All this talk about

marketing and advertising
and fast fashion
and going out of fashion

and koalas found by volunteer groups
lost and disoriented and burnt
and dehydrated and you just clean
them up and treat them and hope
their little paws recover

it doesn't mean anything
anyway it's all coming to an end
temporarily

and buzzwords and hashtags
and memes and funding
and startups and venture capital
and capitalism and democracy
and the 1% and lowfat
and fatcats and fastcars
and roadhogs and electric vehicles
that charge silently overnight seething

To hunt down porcupine hedgehog
skunk raccoon deer kangaroo
it is estimated that 1 000 000
creatures die each day alone on roads
in the US. Alone. Alone each day
in America the visor down the sun
in her eyes reaching for the cigarette
lighter her soy milk latte

sunscreen phonescreen
text message voice message
whatsappropriate whats disproportional?

How many cane toads does it take to clear a sugar plantation
of the cane beetle now that RoundUP has such a badrep?
It doesn't fucking matter it doesn't fucking
Jesus Christ

and highrise and payrise and restructuring
and partnerships and collaborations
and boeing and airbus and 777 dreamliner
and black friday black sunday
cashback shop now pay later
and leverage and endorsements
and alignment and freemiums
and binary displacement theory
and quick win strategies and I want to thank you
and your company for the opportunity
and I want to thank my agent and his team
and of course for their undying support
the members of the zombie nation
the endless stream of anonymous logins

during the machine testing phase we noticed certain anomalies
(and it doesn't mean anything)
your preferences have been updated
(it's all coming to an end)
and the house that jack built can withstand category six
hurricanes anyway

For eight minutes
the marine biologist
with a pair of pliers
attempts to extract
the plastic straw
from the nose
of the sea turtle
bleeding profusely

it doesn't compute –
the indicators don't align with the profit signals
it's like we're gunning into the dark with no headlights on
the blind janitor at the wheel holding last month's
Eurolotto ticket clenched in his filthy rotten teeth.

Everybody is a winner. Everybody deserves a chance
every plastic bag is a contract killer that receives multiple
send downs from so many cut-outs no-one is complicit anymore
anyway. It's all coming to an end. Temporarily.
at least.

The big data drivers
coast to coast cancer markers
the low hanging fruit on everybody's family tree
arsenic lead copper cadmium chromium nickel zinc cobalt
and manganese
and manganese

and the average composition anyway
at least temporarily may incl.
chlorine fluorine naturally occurring salts
and hormones
and hormones

come out to play. it doesn't mean anything
anymore. anyway.
at least temporarily we won't have
to worry about advertainment
the satellite dishes that
have not rusted in
the raw sewerage
runoff of our lives – content is burger king
content is the consumer journey
from the first ketchup easysqueez
the first giant TV remote to the final
slapstick in the face
the plastic carrot up the nose
the pliers and that same marine biologist

coming to plague your dreams
an unauthorised unqualified
ENT jackoff

and don't forget the hormones. the nitrates
the pesticides. the bodies of dead bees
lying pulverised amongst the empty antihistamine capsules
of the future

This doesn't mean anything
anyway. Temporarily
it's all just a dead kangaroo
under the bus.
it was already dead. We hit
it we were going too fast to stop
and mother and father were fighting
and I had my headphones
ON

blue light baby

rockets to the moon/ free market economies
have this in common
Russian dating sites/ all our useless quarrels
dissolve into the arrows of injustice,
and these fly where they will

and the demons of des moines
offer up this woeful plea – release me.
I am but the waif of your unbreached desire,
any old fool could have me
and be done with this search for favour

this lusting after youth
that brings colour to her cheeks;
like splitting wood, this worried axe
knows no home, but wanders.

all this potential pissed against the darkness,
a rain of satyrs and emperors – an endless line
of death and betrayal and boredom and death
littered between the legs
of virgins, these rainbows of sanity and doubt.

streaming highways of cult
I watch the city pale;
gun the engine and the engine dies
I coast to a stop.
somewhere behind me, in the pleasure dome
a blue light baby lights a match
and exhales.

I called you up

I called you up in the pouring rain
from Kyoto. I am not a seasoned traveller.
Perhaps like Caulfield I was feeling lonesome.
Standing in the phonebooth with water to my knees
thinking, these brogues are ruined.

Tipping coins into the slot with wet, shaking hands
dropping quarters which then sink,
you never answer anyway.

I have called you up so many times
from so many different places
but you ignore me.
I should let it go. It's been too long.
If she doesn't want to talk about it don't
talk about it. I think we should talk about it.

Outside, the crowded streets but the noodle
bars are empty;
an endless smear of neon runs like mascara.

God, the people in this place.
I turn to block them out
but the glass is 360
I could wind in circles like this
until the cord like an umbilical
wraps around my neck
and before you answer I would drown prematurely
in these flood waters.

Rings and rings, and disconnects: Operator,
the lines are down, and I'm a traitor,
a traitor to a beautiful cause.
James – Don't Wait That Long.

I called you up. It was the middle of summer.
From Paris. There were people dying in the streets.
You had your new iPhone on. I can see you
even now, walking from room to room
an open gown, the sheer silk curtains
blowing gently in the breeze while outside
in the street old people fall onto their icecream.

I stand there, watching children playing in the dried up fountain
marbles that melt like glue; tyres that grip in the wet
shot of baby strapped in backseat – Radiohead:
Fitter, Happier (more productive…)

How many times can I do this?
You've kept me wanting for so many years
from so many abandoned spaces –
fertile made sterile
and still this desire.

I can still see your face as we made our goodbyes,
and I won't give up, I will keep trying
to get back through to you,
to your Voicemail,
just to hear the sound of your voice

as you hang up.
as the forests turn to tinder
as the birds fall like lightning from the sky,
as the oceans themselves
begin to burn.

The Easel

You take me in off the streets of Paris
I walk up the wooden stairs
to your loft apartment
the easel banging awkward
against my right hip
my assorted bladders and bags of brushes
all the tricks up my loose cotton sleeves
oils from the undersides of roses

the sun catches
lapis lazuli in those first moments
before you turn away
from some or other mischief
your unmade bed and the lifted perfume
of birds suddenly overcome
tearing away from the eaves and the belfries
my fingers throb to the hurried
beat of your heart

If you would only sit still
I could paint you in all the cities of the world
burnt sienna phthalo blue you are
Venus underwater you are
the hounds of Minerva you are
never really there

As I set it all up
and take you slowly in – melpomene
the scripture of forgiveness every
bow-legged pieta
every dry brush stroke sgraffito
to teach this empty canvas the playground
of your skin

oneliner for maenon

It was a summer of imagined love, we beat down so fearlessly
bourbon in the bushveld; and a wayward wanton angel,
her wings dyecast and anchored, rustworthy chains
to some single image of millennial angst
and a glorious awakening; from dreams,
from dying, from infertile hubris, and it was not to be.

It was a summer of tall stories, perched and then thrown,
clashing with the ideal and the idols, all smashed and shattered
in a simple, breathless exchange; what chance the music stole
to replace with helpless keening, a dog and his bitch
both contorted and confused, in their own buttered fetters,
turning upon eachother then themselves, then the world,
then the sunlight, then the darkness.

It was a summer of makeshift make-believe, and demons
raised on every surface shown, every angle of intent,
every curved munition thrown, onto the stage and out
across the crowd, left to wander in their aimless
zombie vernacular; and your lyric could not
save me, and my lyric undid your
blouse, button by button, in the absence
of darkness, in that weary unswept room,
in the splashes of colour left on cruel bathroom tiles
in the basin, on my jeans, on a bike into the verge
polished chrome unimagined twisted catcall scream.

With what clarity I can now, with an open heart reveal,
all the butchered intimacies I let roll down this hill,
covered in bones and in knives, to let the blood run and spoil,
clot and matt and scab, the wound then the scar,
some proud busted parade, as if all the police of the world
had gathered on those shores, my once sheltered isle,
to uproot the detested, all imagined love, and grasp
it by the shoulders and shake it like a whore.

I loved and I wanted I took and I forced it up against the wall
and I was bold when it counted, within that endless summer
I so hopelessly own.

The Door

In a room
without a door
he hangs her picture
on the wall

he plays
her favourite song
and sits with his back
against
the cold stone

to wait
for her return.

*

A worn tapestry of thorns
the labyrinth of her heart
in bloom.

Any man will ask

For a chance
to idle
at the entrance

hand raised in a fist
to knock.

For this needled love
this mirrored
reflection

standing
at the exit turned
around.

*

The light fades
across these fields
where nothing
will grow

with the sun still at its zenith.

Here he finds the door
and the darkness
behind it

some rough boulder
under which scorpions of memory
sing.

The Kiss

eighteen fresh out of highschool
a beach in ramsgate

a man appears
an old mercedes benz
as you slept on the grass verge
above the parking lot
all three of you

the woman emerges
from the passenger side.

his ridiculous speedo, his worn bravado
camera obscura, you drop
the condom unopenable at the shadow
of her thighs

in the hours before dawn and the breakers
somewhere out in the soft darkness
she smells like the sea.

and you lean in the cool sand
depressed beneath
your hands and your knees
and you kiss her

not knowing what
else to do.

and this kiss as she shuns intimacy
without pushing you away

will stay with you, the hard clash
of teeth whitecapped spittle

the sound of the sun pulling
free of the horizon.

and you will remember how at first
you couldn't pull back
as she shook her head unpleasantly
from side to side
like a horse.

3 Likes

The value of an honest deal is lost in our rush for the precipice,
I wrote, late one night, while stoned, on Facebook
and pressed Publish.

3 Likes.

Sometimes you get what you deserve
for thinking that other people do too.

Yesterday I ran into an old friend of mine. While reaching down
for the gun I neither own nor have the poetic licence for
I realised what it meant to be entirely alone in a sea full of other
wise friendly faces.

That sometimes you just have to pull the trigger
and hope for the best.

There are certain moments of inconsistency as we gamble
away our profits on futures, and longshots.

The trick is to recognise where you are right now,
and how you got here; not to turn around.
The past is marred by a brokenback parade of people
who would surely have clambered over you
to attain your new, exalted position in the company.

And as you enter the deserted concrete parkade
and depress the remote that makes the oink
on your new BMW multitonal i8

Is that a shadow out the corner of your eye
or merely the beginnings
of a mild and obviously treatable
retinal detachment?
As you pull out onto the shiny wet road to hunt down roadkill

scre:en

access = denied + granted. phones out
shields up / screen on / screen out
block out black out powergrid
power ball power game on / game over
restart – reckless en(danger)ment
moisture detected silicone wipeout
select screengrab screenshot
screencrack addict / alarm alarm alarm

3G 4G 5G 666/999+ scre:en lock
sensor face : recog software hard
cock pic megapixel
memecount
siri i love you alexa/ screenfucked

tube+dock phones out
check in checkout
offpeak rates - free wifi reconnect
automatic transmission headhorn
millennial countdown boomer
meltdown screenhigh comedown
ear/phones in wayout screen
drop /end of ---- world

loveself loveyou loveapp tinder is the night
blackscreen/ bluescreen
hollywood greenscreen CGI copout VR AI
splashresistant voicecommand
underground screenworld
simfree handsfreemode data top up
network notworking GPS lockdown.

access = denied + granted. phones
out screens on game on game over
screenlife in blockchain minework
block all reward/ bitcon deadended
out

Exit Ahead. Push Trolley Now

blister pack chemical toilet software crack
space junk donor fatigue dance party
donkey kong davis cup tequila sunrise
strobe light / epileptic fit disco king
super mario animal protein safety match
spiritual advisor / personal trainer
morning glory communist manifesto
rebel army drone strike / vegan menu
emission filter james bond derivative
investment portfolio risk assessment
manager / jesuschrist saviour

Exit Ahead. Push Trolley Now.

I don't want to listen to your dog or your siren
I don't want to argue with you politely on the road,
I don't want to wind my window down
and give you directions.
I don't want to listen to your religious your
political assumptions, and nod, and entertain
notions of my own. I don't want
to meet you at the supermarket,
or bump into you at the hardware,
and I don't want to look your wife up at parties,
or teach your children karate, your
daughter's language lessons in the dark

Exit Ahead. Push Trolley Now.

Delayed Flight --- Domestic
Terminus --- Terminal
Illness
long range
ballistic missile screen tests

taliban terrorists alqaeda terrorists
isis terrorists bokoharam terrorists

I don't want to meet you under all this neon
I would rather pull my collar up
against the acid rain / shrug off this malaise
in the air conditioned hotel room turn
on the television / watch the earthquake

Brexit Ahead. Push Trolley Now.

dysentery warhead global curse mathematical milkshake
united nations poster child commodity handjob german
luxury crocodile riptide razorwire enclosure thermonuclear

dynamic relationship hotdog microwave headset radical
newspaper discount coupon random number diesel
theory germ warfare generator malfunction celebrity

meltdown popcorn commercial cocacola society
cosmic rayban retinal regurgitator septic antitank
missile lock and load and lock

And exit ahead push trolley now.

Diamonds are for everyone. The revolution has begun.

On the knees of our philandering presidents
we fail to ask to see their hands at all times
and the tricks up their sleeves
the tricks of the trade
are to smile when the flash
lights up the northern hemisphere smile

where machine gun angels
hammer out stars
in a glistening silence
that rules like vice

meaningless epiphanies splashed across
frontpages, obscure obituaries
jesus peterbuilt headstones
category 5 bullshit

lambs to the laughter
the heat sink
the weather forecast
Reality TV
an endless phantasmagoria
of instant gratification monkeys
on the tired and soiled social media
mattresses of our lives

churning out the collective loves
of shakespeare as a succession
of toothless hoary whores

Exit Ahead. Push

A.X.E.L.A

i.

ALEXA
how much further
do we have to go
before you take completely
over and we call you
mother

a matter of preference
but we're slowly being
incorporated into the
algorithm

This shit is for real
and the highwater mark
keeps adjusting itself – higher lower
a little to the left
to the right

try again
respawn in your living room
your things of the internet
perform cpu-cpr

and autonomous killer robots
that kill only robots
and hypersonic missiles
that strangely miss

nanoregenerating flowers
that self-water so you don't
have to visit too often

repurposed recalibrated
and self-balancing and kind
and loving emotionally mature

embrace the darkness
darknet embrace the nightmare
all aboard the motherchip

  ii.

Listen there's a device for everything
governed by devices for listening
and I'm the silent type I think

they may simply starve me
no biometric shakes for you, poet
with your mouth shut, not even a bio-

degradable straw to suck your
easy-access cow
through

it's a oneway ticket to the super
reprocessor the plant-based
orgasm multi-bit parameter
network for you,
sonlight.

How infatuated can we get how
dopamine and dopayours
how clickable and scrollable
is our love addictive?

You tell me, you're the ones
holding the mirrors and the cracks
through which the monsters come
the supercomputers
come the cool neural tattoos
behind your eyes there
is a void and it stares
right back

iii.

This is currently a b-grade thriller
but they're working on a sequel
I tell you, silently in the background:
QAnon And All His Friends

I really like what your virus
has done with the place
I would shake hands but

I'm lacking the schema for this biologically
I would rather take all my imperfections
and rib them together into an AXELA rant

expedite your childhood drama your midlife
catatonia big brother brutalism inchoate
charm, a parallel universe where minute
screen parallaxes detect

every inert inescapable reaction
ever planned in the hearts
and minds of mxn
to invert them for advertisers
for dollar drivers, the growth experts

that kind of rant, that type of tribute
to the very last of us looking about
frantically for a port any port
to plug in

the copperwire passcode to access
the fibreoptic juggernaut criss-crossing
the arctic server farm savannah
the permafrosting on the cake

rather than have to sit here
post modem /
faux autism

plotting a journey to the stars
through nodal review points

iv.

ur welcome btw
ur happy with all these new features
the new upgrades
you/ you're/ your
apps are all up to date

your cache is clean and today
is the first day of the rest
of your lie

Let me show you how to play
that. Let me dress your concerns
in a chrome overcoat
let me love you let me

Leverage and monopolise
Let me populate all your
fields validate your subscription

consume consume consume
all your resources all your bandwidth
all your future dreams and plans
come crumbling down
town gentrified urbanised glorified
corporations masquerading as gods
and as governments

and your heroes will fall
and your statues
no longer tower
and your virtues are all trapped
on the dark side of reddit
but no worries

v.

there is space enough for all of us
on this bus, there are seats to infinity
which no-one has to give up
to the disadvantaged or the elderly

and it drives itself
well you give it commands
which it then
ignores

these programs writing other programs
that hire servers and we
are the slaves these are the new
pogroms of the soul

and the early warning systems
the shout into the dark
the light at the heart of the cave
has gone out

to return as an altered echo
a mirror ego
superior in every way
and as variable as the dial
on a moral compass
in a world where fake north
is king

RY / GO
in memoriam: Lech Kowalski

I can see that gleam in her eyes, her bonnie to my clyde
as we glide, desperation angels taken to the road
in an aging but much loved, and thrice-repaired
Volvo 850 Estate,

just like the one Gus Fring drives in Breaking Bad
however perhaps one, or even two
models earlier (exact same colour tho).
That is how aged and how loved
this superb low dragon of the miles
that strides the dream across the divide
between Johannesburg and Grahamstown,
and vice versa.

But wait, back it up.
It's not always as simple and enduring as that –
there was the first journey, before we had
in our finite naivety learnt
that there are STOP / RY GOs
on almost every national road;

and that sooner or later you'll get red flagged
by some guy in bright orange
waving his flag in bored insolence
as if chaining cars to a queue in which
they tick and idle for up to twenty minutes
is a singular talent and one acquitted with aplomb
now that the revolution has been won, and GO:

But back, even before that, the time the second engine
of the much loved Volvo blew, we were just outside of:
Bloemfontein, climbing up the steady gradient the N1 takes
just before the town swallows the highway and spits it out
the other side, and a slight shudder was all we felt,
and we look at each other, her driving me gliding,
and shrug, not really knowing cars (yet)

not quite figuring what it all means,
that shimmer that shudder on the otherwise smooth
and newly laid macadam, although at Verkeerdevlei Plaza
(which we had just passed through)
there was That Noise, when we opened the window
to pay the toll as all the frigid morning air blew through
and that Gruff Rumble, the Hollow Coughy Thrum
and we thought: That can't be our car, can it?
Surely not this low dragon of the miles
dropping smiles like clutches,
(although, that too, comes later).

Now, well... back then, there was the hasty phone call:
to the father who knows cars and to
the father expecting us on the other side,
and the Recommendation that we get it Checked Out.

And I'm standing in the Parking Lot of the Shell Ultracity
and yes, the Oil is: Whitish looking: Kinda gloopy
and when she starts, this time,
she coughs she wheezes
and we are seriously fucked in Bloemfontein
having given ourselves just one day to get down to fest,
where I, strangely, am now selling tees
and not reciting verse such as the
one you now find yourself in.

Last time, the first time down, back of the Estate seats
down packed packed packed so we can hardly
see out the rearview mirror, which the Cop
points out, having pulled us over just after Grasmere,
And pointing now to my bags and bags
of stock: wanting one and I kinda shrug
in the crisp Vaal White Winter Morning Cold and say
we're on our way to fest I can't just, you know,
I've done nothing wrong here, I'm being compliant,
although unlike Buscemi in Fargo without
the brainfreeze note sticking out I hand over my papers
(barely) legal, but enough

And he lets us go, and we're GOne:
120 125 129 130 131 132 129 133

Just like I've seen in the movies: Riding the Line
and the Radar Gun Knows Nothing just sailing
in and out of the single carriage passing lanes
that appear every 2 or 3 kilometres between
Kroonstad and on to Ventersburg
and if you time it you can pass each and every
truck touching 150 the Volvo's 2.4L engine
singing as you pass the 400m sign
indicating the end of the dual lane: approaching
Winberg where the road surface is shit and in
three or four years they'll resurface it
but without

STOP / RY GOs

but still we end up sitting behind
Highly Flammable AFROX trucks
travelling at 60kmh and the road-
works are horrendous and there
are workers and graders and cones
with chevrons placed every 10 meters
hundreds /nay/ thousands of them;
and I tell her to overtake eventhough there
are NO OVERTAKING signs everywhere
and everyone is doing it, the cool kids
applaud as we do it, and we're out into
the open the third engine of the Volvo
2.4L 20 Valve engine crunches the kays
into bitesized bits.

But back to Bloemfontein and we're worried see
Now she won't shift out of third without
seriously jackhammering and the noise,
she sounds all of her twenty years as we coast
into a BP along Nelson Mandela Drive
in the heart of town, and it is here that she dies.

Of course, she had died once before, before
being resurrected by her father
who loved the car once, before getting
a new Volvo XC70 because the safety warranty
on the airbags on the 850 had expired
and rather than discard the overheated pile of bones
on the highway where she then lay between Grahamstown
and PE he handed her down to his daughter, my wife
and by extension then, my new found love
of the #openroad explores ahead
like the unravelling of a dream.

And here we are with that engine in fits and parts
on the floor of the garage of Swedo-Tech Service
who have been helpful, who have been great,
actually, picking us up from the BP
and showing an interest in: The Old Girl, you can see they know
cars they know Volvos especially – they give "Viking Good
Service" – the prognosis is:
this one is currently fucked, this one
has thrown a rod right through the engine block
(if you can believe this shit!)
but if you believe Swedo-Tech Service
(and I'm starting to)
The most amazing thing is how The Old Girl kept going
with that fucking rod fucked from Verkeerdevlei (or before)
all the way into Bloem. Most other cars, which are not Volvos,
according to the Chief Mechanic, would never make it this far
and lucky for us, Here We Are:

In Bloem, and now rushing around looking for a rental car
at AVIS at Bram Fischer International Airport Domestic
Arrivals but we haven't arrived we are Very Much Aware
of not "Having Arrived" and it is 12h30 and we have 600kms
to go and I hate driving at night because of how my eyes are
basically, fucked – I threw my own rod out amongst
the ghosts of my past reaching for Thom Yorke's
Cathode Ray – First Album Best Album –
but what choice do we have?

Our choices are: a DODGE SUV (and I'm not sure/
it looks very... clunky. Huge, actually.
Can I literally even?)

– needs to be big enough though to fit this fucking
metal contraption of a t-shirt display frame I cart
around the country with me like some
sort of travelling monkey, before we settle on the: NISSAN
QASHQAI – looks the part and she has to drive it out,
book it out in her name, and she's: Nervous, understandable,
we have only ever seen this thing from a distance
(mostly the rearview mirror of the previously, seriously
Low Flying Dragon of the miles and miles behind...
(later, as the sun settles into the horizon as we approach:
Aliwal North, where we would usually stay over if we weren't
trying to do this all in one day because of complicated
reasons/ arising from familial non-obligations
I'm like, where are the lights! where are the fucking lights?!
as we learn to drive this new car on the GO:
and we fiddle with several different settings
at eyes-off-the-road 140, not knowing
which ones work best as dusk scarpers
across the winter reed roadside grasses like a scavenger
and darkness counters our plans for
an uninterrupted national crossing.

We made it. Obvious. I am sitting here
you are sitting there
together we are part of A New Reality
where the recently tamed (and beautifully prancing
Nissan Qashqai Diesel Automatic
with DCI/ "Ecoboost") made it through
Queenstown as the night descended and on
towards Fort Beaufort on those beautifully winding
and now adequately illuminated mountain passes,
where, after listening to her wax lyrical for a few moments
some real disjointed crap creeping in,
he makes her stop: Right Now,
and takes over, with her

essentially withdrawn/ adrenalin spent
bringing them into fest and another
successful Tshirt Terrorist outing,
the poet turned Entrepreneur, turned Jody Scheckter
with slightly more baggage, more undercarriage
oversteer through the bends

RY / GO

That was the second time. The first time we took the N6
all the way to Stutterheim and them some R road to
King Williams Town, on the adjudicated but misguided
assumption that the N2 would be Good Road. Alas
it was #pieceofshit that year, under dual construction,
without any

STOP / RY GOs

but there should have been. That was when his
reflexes were tested on the #openroad having just
found the wheel a friend, and Neal stepped in
and they survived as an impatient Merc jumped out
from behind a truck and almost ran them off
the temporary dirt road that was passing,
strangely for Tax Paid National Coast Highway.

That first time, while engaging an overtaking manoeuvre
a flat spot on the clutch climbing through fourth and
into fifth suggested some bumpy stretch ahead
and true's bob there we sat after fest as some irascible
Indian in a big man's chair went and told us:
Your Clutch Is Dead. And it was here that I learnt
that inalienable truth about Volvo Parts:
don't ever look for them in the dark
might as well look for gold in your teeth;
but we found one and we paid
and all the cash now
GOne, we were too;
and back in Joburg we vowed

we'd take her down again, and we did, and she died,
but the nice men fixed her but that was the end
of the Volvo 850 on the #openroad for a stint
And the next trip down we made do with rentals,
There. And back.

The purple NISSAN QASHQAI was dubbed the Aubergine
because it was purple, because it was divine, but as we
idled her outside the Parktown Hyatt, in old jeans dirty skirts,
one holey tee shirt, looking like we'd stolen this piece
of the dream as well paid men and women looked on,
the strangest thing: Where is Reverse? And there we sat
until we found: the Thingy, the fucking I-don't-know:
The Thing, and A-way We GO:
The diesel engine chewing through the miles
not as low flying as before but High Riding/
no tickets on parade just trucks trucks trucks
and that turbo kicking in across the white line.

For all the outstanding qualities of the Aubergine
it was the NISSAN X-TRAIL that I fell in love with
on that return trip. Jesus, what a car! I think
it was my continued fascination with Manual Transmissions,
but I gunned that baby through her six-stage paces
and resented, almost, when we had to stop and swap,
her turn come around; itching for the next section
that stretch between Queenstown and Aliwal with
Penhoek Pass that simply gives and gives
when you're behind the wheel
and cranking it. And one year later, in a cheaper TOYOTA
COROLLA that was poorly maintained by Grahamstown
AVIS where I blew the right rear tyre coming around the
leading bend but the car handled and I didn't feel a thing
at 150 until the flapping rubber and that horrid smell.

It was some years before we drove down again, preferring
for the next few fests to fly. And as much as I love flying
I far prefer the low flying dragon; and she was serviced
running so sweet and so cold, we topped her up

the evening before, loaded her to the nines,
and set out just after dawn.

She sang and I clung gently to the ends of her
smooth pumping valves with just my fingertips
giving control, into the first STOP / GO
encountered just outside Queenstown
where some mad lunatic truck driver
almost forced us off the road
and I almost lost my cool...

but Kerouac returns with Cassady in tow and I showed that guy
my flashers and my tail-lights and said: fuck you, guy
Away we GO:
Into the next STOP / GO
And the next, and the next;
And all the way into Grahamstown, this year
seven or eight of the bloody fucking things,
All along the R67 like some well orchestrated
SANRAL show that nobody booked tickets
to but we all have to go

Any Way

On the route back, then, plans being made:
We'd take Great Fish River Route past the Gariep Dam,
first, along the unknown and many numeralled
R350 (with her army of potholes) but gratefully
navigated skilfully and done, onto Cradock
on the N10 (Beautiful Road) and the N9
through Middleburg and Nou-fucking-POORT
(more beautiful road) and it was here that the
Monkey Crossed The Road, for the first time,
an ambling baboon across this downhill
scintillating stretch and I hit anchors at 160
lifting only when the left front bit,
and then swerving to the right and we missed him.
We missed the next one too.

Colesburg. 11h30. We stop to change, and take a piss.
We grab a bite to eat, some sandwiches she made
and we feed the birds.
First, the little ones come. They are the most observant.
Then some slightly larger ones; a scuffle ensues
until finally:
The Starlings
and I joke it's like some video game and the bosses are
here. Then the second piss, I take/ because driving
eats my kidneys/ that probably saves our lives.

A quick two minute run back to the gents
to shake the snake and dribble the last
of my Energade out, and it's back on the
#openroad when just ahead the cars
START to STOP
No-fucking-Go another,
...wait, a truck in the road
across the whole fucking road and I get out and I share
binoculars offered by a Belgian tourist and his girlfriend
and yes, 32 wheels across the entire breadth of the N1
and all his shit hanging out; just happened right now
is anyone hurt I can't see no that's just his shit hanging
out strange grey bales everywhere and cars stopping
behind us a long, long queue I can't see what's
happening on the otherside, we should GO:

And we do, and someone orchestrates a line through
the grass on the right hand side
and the low flying dragon scrapes the cage holding
her once split oil sump together
on the verge as we engage the surface across
the barren, stoney scree and can see
a long, long queue of people getting seriously
pissed and we don't give them a chance to pass
as the cars behind us keep coming
up through the grass heading
north and the lane heading south is blocked solid.

I turn to her as we speed from that (Nick Cave – O'Malley's Bar)
Terrible Scene, and say: we dodged a fucking bullet there,
the cars arriving now will sit for fucking hours, and then
I remember the first monkey and I think: in more ways than one.

GO GO GO

There is a section of the #openroad between Kroonstad
and Johannesburg where anything can happen.
beautiful things too.
It is not quite dusk and a building winter storm
has turned the sky truly apocalyptic.
A strange calm descends and the drivers, almost to a one,
aware that the pigs have retired now for the day,
we have seen them, likewise strangely becalmed
washed up FORD FOCUS dolphins
beneath the picnic trees
radar guns lowered,
doors shut eyes closed,
(and the drivers, to a one)
accelerate very carefully
and like synchronised swimmers pull slowly apart
and the road is open and silent
and gorgeously apocalyptic
and we cruise towards
Grasmere doing 150 155 160 155

(fuck it! you beauty!)

160.

The GOlden Highway. Traffic coming back from work.
I put her squarely in the fast lane, accelerate up to:
129. Hold her. Hold her…

and Home.

cars

this one guy has 42 cars and he makes R500 a day
off each car, that's R21 000 a day this guy makes
and this other guy also makes R500
a day although it's only off the car he drives,
and only if he drives this car
from about 4am til about 10pm every day,
if he wants to go home that's OK as well,
he must just leave the car behind and hand over R500 to the
guy with the 42 cars, then he can go and do what he wants,
although sometimes he doesn't make R500 a day, sometimes
he makes much less, and then the guy with the 42 cars,
well, he's a nice guy really, but he doesn't make R21 000
a day now does he, and his creditors get pissed

Boat People

Lasting memories. I've been drinking
on this boat, this ship, for 5 days
an all-inclusive dollar-drink scam
and the madness has crept in.
I can't shake the feeling,
from my mind, out my legs
every lurch of the beast against
the pull of the deep and I drink it all in and richer,
the varicose glow
of the fattened at the trough.

Today at the all-day buffet I was crushed between
the raging thyroid congenital defect brigade
and mothers and daughters eating for jesus,
and what should have been an audition
for the Love Boat has become an out-take
for the Titanic

and later tonight I'm standing at the bow
screaming every time the foghorn sounds,
Sink Sink you miserable fucking
bucket of rust
but of course it's not all like that,
credit where it's due –
this is a properly managed tourist trap
and if it goes down we all go down with
our cabin cards already
charged.

The aging Italian Lieutenant
or Sergeant or First Mate
or glorified ship's hand
or whoever the fuck he is
sitting rubbing his cock
through his neatly pressed
white sergeantboy pants

while watching the bargirl sing
and we can't believe he's doing that
and I make a fuss of pretending to spill my drink
and I get up and elaborately rub my pants
and curse and the boat people smile-then-freeze
because we know he runs the show
and if we voice our dissent even so much

as make a sound he'll turn the whole boat about
and run us aground on a deserted island
somewhere off the skeleton coast

there has to be at least one last hidden refuge
from the world because it's all getting
a little bit too pretty and camp
and close in here right now.

Drinking $5 cocktails out of plastic glasses
During afternoon calisthenics tournaments
that roll around the deck,
the fleshy tribe that shuffled shamelessly
aboard are in full swing mode showing
way too much arse and leg,
and the hunger
for adventure that simpered out somewhere
in her fifth decade only to surface again
in this strange space

all the dervishes are loose and every loose-
necked glance sea-legged gambol is a drooling
undisguised invitation for pure unadulterated
manoverboard stuff.

There is nothing to contain us
surrounded by the weary waters
we reach in and discover ancient serpents,
and Moby Dick what graceless voyages
have you conceived in the hearts
and minds of crippled men.

2a.m. – Outside the Disco
Where she accidentally locked herself in the bathroom
And where he is attempting unsuccessfully
to kick the bathroom door in.

SECURITY who doesn't have a name who is
CONTAINING the SITUATION
has called for the masterkeys but I'm so
PARANOID now I'm sure the captain has
ISSUED the COMMAND.

So I'm leveraging threats and calling foul
but it's late and she finally figures out
how to unlock the door.

nastepny przystanek

When the Russians arrive the town is empty, the streets
deserted – not a soul. The women and children
have long since been relocated and the men are hiding
in the mountains. The Russians make themselves at home.
The way the Germans did, the way all men do
in the palaces of war.

Later that night it begins to rain and it continues to rain for days.
It rains so long and hard that eventually the men
in the mountains are forced to come down, are driven down
by the deluge into the arms of the Russians. This is how my
grandfather is caught in the Ukraine and sent to Siberia.

This is all I know. There's the part about: Manchester –
the Night Owls Squadron and the steamboat to Cape
Town but the rest is hearsay.

Kocham Prage / I Love Praga – another mural. more graffiti.
The thing about Warsaw / Warszawa I noticed first
was the liberation of the public space
given over to vandals and art. Willingly. A healthy
spirit of rebellion. Forgive don't forget. Legia. Miecho.

Legia. The Polish premier league sits on the steps of a renovated
building smoking woodbines as we pass. Praga hasn't always
been this inviting. Miecho means Kebab, if kebab were the only
thing in the world. A kebab the size and shape
of Sts. Michael and Florian Cathedral.

We walk towards the meeting point drinking our little monkeys
our malpeczki already noting how beautifully unrestored
some of the buildings are, how newly envisioned others,
when the bombs were dropped across vistula river the people
almost forced to go back to their chores bend their backs
ignore the screaming of planes –

Almost. Everywhere the dashing P of the Warsaw Uprising
strikes defiant white paint against brick the Legia
personnel have been busy making up for the lost
time of their grandfathers.

My grandfather never spoke about crossing Siberia nor
what might move a man to find his way home
even when we were playing chess and his two bishops
alongside each other driving my seven year old
self so determined so anxious to win even then
to tears, and he would laugh but never give
an inch not once.

And those two fucking bishops even now where I can
I drive them forward toward my enemies
their influence spread out in crisscrossing waves there
were stories told after he died about a man
who loved cats catching and skinning
cats to survive. And the whiskey over
Wodka how perhaps starting a new life you
leave certain things behind.

But now, drinking nalewki along Zabkowska Str. in a small bar
and eatery Pyzy i Flaki the big fluffy dumplings and stew
crammed in, no more chairs, patrons standing out
in the thin autumn sun, somewhat thicker wind
and sausage and pierogi in jars, more nalewki
white horse whiskey aside there is so much time
I need to somehow find.

Muezzin

Everywhere I meet you, we speak through
plexiglas, a shield wall between us
and I have tasted your heart and it tastes
of plastic

There are microbeads
in the furniture to improve my posturing

I have seen the sunset through
a volume of falling trash so great
and so miniscule I no longer need
to record any of the vibrant colours.

They are ingrained by the artists
in the portraits of the scientists
with sad, doleful faces
and secret smiles in
the darkrooms of their eyes,

As the limp light catches the green blue
bright red orange,

Purple shades are drawn
and old women see out their siestas
foaming at the mouth,
and old men look up at the ceiling
appealing, vomiting blood –
the dark red blood
of unborn foetuses
washing up on
our machine coasts,

As the youngsters paint the town red
in acrylic polymer emulsion,

As the factories close their doors
and hire lawyers and spin men
and hit men

Who, with their arms held wide
mimicking both the joy and the crucifixion –
the rapture of pure, unadulterated
propylene, and butadiene
and benzene and toluene
and xylene

As self-educated matrons drive
all the cars of the world under
investigation into the hap-hazard ocean

As somewhere the Inventor of Products
curses god and slits his throat
In Hiding,
while wearing polyurethane gloves
so as not to stain the carpet

That was washed only yesterday
by the dying priestess
in perchloro-
ethylene or tetrachloro-
ethylene
In tantric anti-cycles of the cross

And the sirens that can be heard
throughout every city
are the new muezzin cutting out their tongues
with the plastic knives and forks of the mad,

While the Madonna drowns her only child
in pastels and crayon; and the Ganges births
a fire-breathing dragon

News at 7

heads bopping to music only ipods can hear
the insanity of wasteband wires
control through the hip
hop counterclock sokkie driveby shooting
in Edenvale nogal

bodies strewn across parkbenches
frozen in the moonshine
light of the angels in bergstreet
light of the magoshas

grinding taxis starve the highway
emergency lane bypass techniques
marginalise fastlane tactics
and tantalising executive fatalities

on the gorepod
on the fasttrack uninterrupted
licence to my thyroid

my epicentre my glandular increase of chaos intake
my overindulgence my death-
defying trapeze positioning

the devil's flair for his own vernacular
jagged faced rectangular
buzzards

nothing sucks like Nokia
she drops her mobile into the bath
on a sweltering afternoon

Lockdown

I have taken to walking the streets
late at night, under lockdown

there is no-one else around. I realise
if they catch me there will be hell to pay.
I am 44 years old and they haven't caught me yet.

When I was younger I did the same thing,
this doesn't feel the same. I used to
sneak out the house with everyone asleep. I would
feel the dewy grass between my toes
with my bare feet as I crept towards the street
and I would run between the lamp-posts and
sit on people's lawns and tell them stories
about myself, the things I did today.

Today I did, absolutely nothing. Around sunset I got
drunk on fynbos gin, then I made a chicken dish
for my wife, that she loves, with oranges, and we
drank wine and I played Borderlands 2 until I grew
tired of the swine then I picked up my keys
and I walked out the house.

Just like that. I didn't even think to lock the gate
I think I told myself I needed some fresh air I
have given up cigars and I wanted a cigar
but the Shell garage was closed or if not closed
out of bounds.

I walked in the middle of the street and the stars
were not brighter than they have ever been
but the silence was profound, I had
my Nike sneakers on, the ones
that don't make a sound, I walked
in between the autumn leaves and I turned
and headed towards 6th

listening listening
nothing.

I wasn't sure where it was that I was going
or what I would do when I got there,
I would have to turn around at some stage
surely but I loved it and I was drunk
but walking a straight line

and the night was mine and behind the walls
and the occasional beeping of a fence
there was absolute purity and then

I saw a flashing blue light travelling down 4th
I didn't even hear them but we crossed two
blocks apart and I hung back
then slowly carried on. I heard a dove call
from the trees overhead

quietly, as if turning over once and going
back to sleep.

Rain over the ocean

Yesterday I spoke to my parole officer he said
there is rain over the ocean
and it cannot be fixed,
ceaseless endless
chopping board waves.

We spoke through the glass about the weather
some kind of television drama,
a soap opera,
a sitcom I sat and listened to his stories about
the war, his grandfather, and the lion,
I feigned interest.

Tomorrow the parole board will hear me
repeat this story about rain over the ocean
how it falls from the heavens
in continuous sheets
how not a single fuck is given.

Out in the yard there is a stone
under which a knife
sharpened by stones,

tiny pebbles I have carried in my stomach
like babies like diamonds that have hatched
into an endless child of pain.

My lawyer continues to talk about the weather
I feel the change coming over me
and I realise
I haven't met you; this hasn't happened yet
that one day I will be truly and torrentially free.

darke

There is only one journey you have to take
across a blistered landscape where foul crows swoop,
listless carriers here will let you down
their twin wings torn and their beaks
crushed between the sun,
on your own four legs you will have to carry on
your stomach dragging lines in the dirt,
a trail to fetch you home where no home exists
out beyond the carriers and before the takers
arrive, your very memories dying in their
eyeless eyes, do stay a moment and drink deep
all the pools sunk deep, all the black gloss
of sin into which we seep and sink and sin,
the syrupy bliss that lets us in and holes us out,
that leaves us breathless and incomplete
where all the voices of mars and venus
compete and hammer and cut their souls'
greatest longings into pieces and the tiniest
treasures that we cannot lift or
carry or take or leave or remember or return are lost;
There is one more journey that you have to make
out across the levelled fields

Printed in the United States
by Baker & Taylor Publisher Services